God, Help My Mind

Darlene Britt

Thanks!

~My Most Sincere And Heartfelt Thanks~

First and foremost to my Lord and Savior, Jesus Christ – to whom I give infinite honor and praise.

To my entire family – I love you so much. A special thank you to Pastor D.L. Greene, my Aunt who raised me and taught me God's Word.

To my church family, Greater Joy Baptist Church, there are no words that can justly express my love for you guys. At the lowest point in my life, it was the preaching of our Bishop, S. C. Daniel that enabled me to push through every obstacle that was in my way. But thank you, God, I'm on my way. Bishop Daniel - much love, honor and respect to you, great man of God.

To Mrs. Rhonda S. Pittman, a very special thank you for your hard work and dedication to making this possible. Love you, Rhonda

To Vicci Van Valen and Virginia G. Jacobs, thanks for your help and support.

To Dr. James R. Davis, my mentor, spiritual guide and my professor of the faith. Thanks for your passion and willingness to share the Word, your Wisdom and patience.

INTRODUCTION

I was prompted by the Holy Spirit to write a Christian Romance/Encouragement book to help guide and encourage those who are in the struggle. I was driven to research, study and learn more about writing, publishing and creating a finished product.

God help my mind!! Single and loving God, does your mind take you there? We can make it by depending only on God, and our desire to obey His Word. Men want a woman they can take home to "Mama", a woman of standard - with morals and high values. I have a unique story. After a failed marriage I found myself in a dilemma to say the least. Finances were not a problem, being a single parent was not a problem, but the companionship piece of my puzzle was missing.

I was walking in a place I had never walked before. I questioned if I was walking on my own or was God carrying me? I had to learn how to cope with emotions and feelings on a different level. When you divorce, you face challenges that NEVER crossed your mind, coupled with emotions that were tied up in the turmoil of a breakup. Some emotions were lying dormant for a while. When they awakened, I wasn't prepared. But with God, I made it and am still making it. Taking the time to heal from hurt and a broken heart has been a roller coaster ride. I pray that this book will be a blessing to you.

God, Help My Mind!
Copyright©2012 by Darlene Britt

Scriptural References taken from the King James Version
The KJV® Bible (The Holy Bible, King James Version®) copyright © 1990 by Thomas Nelson, Inc., a publishing ministry of Thomas Nelson Publishers. KJV® Giant Print Reference Edition: 1990. The KJV ® has been reproduced in cooperation with and by permission of Thomas Nelson Publishers. Unauthorized reproduction of this publication is prohibited. All rights reserved.

The "KJV" are trademarks of Thomas Nelson Publishers.

All rights reserved, no part of this book may be reproduced or transmitted in any form or by any means without written permission from author.

ISBN-978-0-9908510-0-4
Cover art by TyQuarius Pittman
Printed in USA by Createspace
Published by Darlene Britt

TABLE OF CONTENTS

1. God, Help My Mind!
2. Singleness
3. Can't Keep Waiting
4. Being Processed
5. What Is Your Name?
6. Ageless
7. Reward
8. Girl Talk
9. Dos
10. Don'ts

Chapter 1

"God, Help My Mind!!"

What does a Christian of single status have to do with all these desires, passions and images? God made humans above every other creature, so we have to go back to the beginning and look at our makeup. We are awesome and complex people of the Most High (Ps. 139:4). So let's take a deeper look into who we are and find help. God's way is the right way. When we commit to His way, the stronger we become.

Gen. 1:27: *So God created man in His own image, in the image of God created He Him, male and female created He them.*

The Bible states that we were created in the image and likeness of God. We are tri-parti beings, spirit, body and soul. The body is where we function in the natural. Through the soul is where we engage in our relationship with God. Our mind is where our will and emotions dwell. Whatever God makes His, He is well able to take care of. We are a part of Him and in turn, He is our heavenly father.

Gen 2:8 : *And the LORD God planted a garden eastward in Eden, and there He put the man whom He had formed.*

Adam was alone in the garden, God said, "Let us make you a help meet." The garden had everything Adam needed with the exception of one thing--a helper. So God made him a helper, to help him in every area of his life.

Gen 2:21-22 *And the LORD God caused a deep sleep to fall upon Adam, and he slept: and He took one of his ribs, and closed up the flesh instead thereof, And the rib, which the LORD God had taken from man, made He a woman, and brought her unto the man.*

God made woman for Adam. Everything about this woman turned Adam on, so much so he named her, "woo-man". Eve had lips and hips. She was round and ripe - his ideal. You know... that top model woman. In other words, she brought pleasure to Adam.

Gen 2:23 *And Adam said, "This is now bone of my bones, and flesh of my flesh: she shall be called Woman, because she was taken out of Man.*

As Christians, God wants us to have a full and abundant life, physical, social, emotional, and sexual. God is concerned about the whole man, not just the soul of man for they are tied together.

John 10:10: *The thief cometh not but for to steal, and to kill, and to destroy: I am come that they might have life, and that they might have it more abundantly.* God does not want us to go unfulfilled in any area of our lives. It is His plan for us to be complete, whole and live in abundance. He wants us to experience ecstasy. Sex is not a taboo subject for Him, wherein he turns a deaf ear or zones out while sex is discussed. We were placed here to enjoy everything, including each other, in the right context.

If we don't, we live beneath the privilege that God granted us. The Bible says everything God made was good and very good. That, my friend, includes sex. Our bedrooms should be blessed. So don't ask God to remove your desires because you will need them at a later time. (Thank God!) As a single person, there is no doubt that I love Jesus. Yet there are times, and more than occasionally, that my flesh wants to be touched and held.

    Let's not play games. Real talk - even though I try to fight or deny it, it still exists. My mind creates images. This is where I live. If you are honest, you can say me too. Don't get it twisted... I am still saved. Being raised in the old church, you were taught that if you had these feelings, you were not saved. Being saved is not based on feelings, but on our relationship, belief and trust in God. So we beat ourselves up for having desires that are natural... the God-given nature of all mankind.

There is an old saying that says, "Always a bridesmaid, never a bride." Being saved does not mean that our desires will disappear or vanish like the wind. We messed up in the past by trying to deny our feelings - not dealing with our desires and emotions. As soon as he paid us a compliment, it went to our heads and he got the body. It was so easy for him. Amen. Even while praying, thoughts come to mind that we have to rebuke. Praying and pushing to go into the high holies - in the presence of God for help. That's where the enemy does not want you to go. Your adversary wants you to stay weak and vulnerable. Often times we ask ourselves the questions, "What if?" "Why not?" "Am I not good enough?"

The truth of the matter is you could be better off being the bridesmaid and not the bride. Marriage tells the truth – love or lust. Compatibility comes to mind, someone who believes just as you do about God and what He says.

2 Cor. 6:14: *Be ye not unequally yoked together with unbelievers: for what fellowship hath righteousness with unrighteousness? And what communion hath light with darkness?*

All the preparation for the wedding is great, but it is not the marriage. It's after the ceremony that the marriage starts. Marriage in itself is a beautiful thing and instituted by God. Sex should be saved and sanctified for the marriage.

Gen 2:22-24 *And the LORD God caused a deep sleep to fall upon Adam, and he slept: and He took one of his ribs, and closed up the flesh instead thereof, And the rib, which the LORD God had taken from man, made he a woman, and brought her unto the man. And Adam* *said, this is now bone of my bones, and flesh of my flesh: she shall be called Woman, because she was taken out of Man.*

Therefore shall a man leave his father and his mother, and shall cleave unto his wife: and they shall be one flesh.

    Two flesh becoming one is a miracle that only God can bring to pass. This involves two people from different backgrounds, with different values and morals. Both are strong-willed people and trying to have their own way. Both are thinking that their own thoughts and ideas are right, these two that must become one. But it's ok. Leave mother and father and put spouse first in all things. God is the potter and we are the clay. Marriage means being molded and mended together, I would even say woven together. So now the questions become, what do you do when you are not married and hormones start raging? How do you keep it together? You hold it together with the help of the Lord! Only by relying on Him!

Chapter 2

"Singleness"

What a blessing being single is. It means that I have time for God and the things of God. Being single should not imply that I am not whole. It is Christ that makes us whole. So being married is not the key to wholeness. Christ is that key. Singleness also implies that I am strong enough to wait on God's timing. Truth be told, we could all be married. However, there are benefits to being single. You have the freedom to come and go as you please. People frequently imply that something is wrong with you if you are single. Beware, brace yourself for that kind of ignorance. You don't have to defend yourself for being single.

Danny Santagato quote:
*"**Being** single doesn't necessarily mean one is not wanted. In many cases it means that one knows what they want and if they can't find that someone special then they'll remain single forever because they're OK and happy with who they are and just want that someone special to complete them and take their happiness to a higher level[iii]."*

You now have time to plan your life. Write down what it is you want in a mate and start preparing yourself for the relationship in advance. Don't let anybody push you into a relationship that you are not ready for. While waiting pamper yourself to manicures, pedicures, and massages - you deserve it. Enjoy being you. Travel - see the world. After all, there's nothing to keep you from pampering yourself and seeing new and exciting places.

Remember you are single, and it has its advantages. All the freedom in the world belongs to you. The choice is yours. Pick and choose your dates, and whom you date. Please don't choose out of desperation, or the want/need of dating someone. Even if it has been a while sometimes singleness can bring on self-pity. Don't become overwhelmed. Keep the faith - this too will pass. In the meantime enjoy being at peace with who you are. Don't mimic anybody else. Put God first in all you do and allow His will for your life.

God is in control.

Chapter 3

"Can't Keep Waiting"

Many times we look at our present situation, the right here and right now. We begin to pray that God sends us someone and soon. We convince ourselves that we can't continue to wait on the Lord. We begin to doubt that we can practice being of good courage while letting Him strengthen our hearts.

Ps. 27:14: *Wait on the LORD: be of good courage, and He shall strengthen thy heart: wait, I say, on the LORD.*

The word "wait" is mentioned twice in this scripture, which says to me it is essential. The words "old maid" come to mind - meaning that you will be old and set in your ways and no one will want you. That's a trick of the enemy. We have to use wisdom when dealing with our adversary, he is cunning and wise in every way. Remember he is called "the deceiver." Let God strengthen your heart while waiting. Let Him speak to your spirit as only He can.

Eph. 6:11: *Put on the whole armor of God, that ye may be able to stand against the wiles of the devil.*

We need on the full armor from head to toe leaving nothing uncovered to fight in this battle. We need to be fully equipped to fight against the Devil. He has all kinds of tricks and schemes, and might I add, he's been doing it for a very long time! I believe that God has to prepare us for what we think we want. Many times once we get what we want, it becomes a whole different story – we discover that it's not how we always dreamed it would be. Just like the old saying, "Be careful what you ask for - you just might get it!" In your waiting, let God work on the real you. It seems we have a set timeline for things to happen in our lives. For instance, you might say by the time I reach age 25 I want to be married, have my degree and a good job in my field. We need to understand that God has timing for our lives too.

We don't want to be ahead of God - we want to coincide with Him. You and God make a team that cannot be reckoned with. We all have been hurt in relationships, whether it was your first love or your last love. We must be careful not to carry old baggage into a new relationship. Let's ask God to cleanse us from all unhealthy ties of the past. You know, so that we don't compare the new person to the old person. Many times we don't even realize that this is happening.

In a recent conversation, a young lady confided that she has trust issues. She's thinking that every new person will be the same as the old person "Joe", who was a liar and cheater. Because "Joe" lied, it's hard for her to trust again. She added that she really tries not to compare, but it's hard for her not to make those comparisons. She stated, for an example, that she likes how "Mike" would take care of her finances and pay her bills.

It seems like nowadays most guys look for her to cover everything. Even in intimacy she made comparisons, "June Bug" didn't do it the way "Joe" did, etc. So...I asked her why all of her previous relationships ended? Why was she still holding on to the past? Was the problem really all on them - or did she have issues too? Most often we want and even expect the other person to be our "everything." What we need to remember is that only God, Jehovah, can be our "everything". We set ourselves up for disappointment and failures thinking otherwise.

I remember as a little girl the American dream was to get married, have two children, (typically a boy and a girl) and live in a house with a picket fence...wow. If you got married, had two children and a house - that was the life. Now the dream in today's society is to get married and be able to stay together! The divorce rate is just as high in the church as it is in the secular world.

While we are single, we can work on ourselves. We can work on getting rid of everything that will keep us from being "one" with our mate. While waiting for your mate, keep working to make yourself the "Best You". Keep waiting and let *patience* have her perfect work.

Patience is referenced as "feminine" in nature, meaning her characteristics are delicate and conceivable. We can obtain and achieve patience. When we speak that we can't wait for something, it gets in our spirit. The Bible says, "Out of the heart, the mouth speaketh, life and death are in the power of the tongue." Let's look at it.

Chapter 4

"Being Processed"

The meaning of process: *to treat or prepare by some particular procedure - as in manufacturing or to handle systematically, organizing things, following up with appropriate actions or the like. Also: operation, process, procedure, proceeding to apply to something that goes on or takes place, a process of series of progressive and interdependent steps by which an expected end is obtained.*

According to the Word of God, it is not meant for man to be alone. Your adversary, the devil, uses that to beat up on us. He taunts us with it and speaks to us through images that are so strong, they stick in our minds and we have to pray: **God help my mind!** The process will help you with being unsure of what you really want, to really know what you are willing to accept or not accept. For instance, you date someone who has children... are you willing to love them as your own? Sometimes we feel as though we are ready now and can't wait. There are other times we feel as though we are not ready yet and we need time to get a handle on our emotions and get things in order.

Being processed helps to get this perspective in order.

Phil. 4:11-13: *Not that I speak in respect of want: for I have learned, in whatsoever state I am, therewith to be content. I know both how to be abased, and I know how to abound: everywhere and in all things I am instructed both to be full and to be hungry, both to abound and to suffer need. I can do all things through Christ, who strengthens me.*

Paul says, "I have learned whatever state I am in, to be content." He (Paul) learned to reshape his thoughts and come into the knowledge of the truth. When we change our thinking, our faith rises. If you wander around and around, you'll never grow up spiritually, causing you to ***never*** enter into the destiny that God has ordained for your life.

Discontentment will keep you where you are. Be strong wherever you are.

Strong in the way you think, strong in your frame of mind. God will strengthen your mind.

2 Cor. 10:5: *Casting down imaginations, and every high thing that exalteth itself against the knowledge of God, and bringing into captivity every thought to the obedience of Christ.*

Every high thing is whatever consumes the majority of your time, and/or takes priority over present situations. In the relationship, there is always one common denominator - you. You, by far, are the easiest factor to change. So weigh the pros and the cons and change your thinking. This is part of your "P.O." also known as "Process Out". When you learn to cast down every high thing that is exalting itself in your life, you are on your way to taking that thing captive, meaning you are in control with the help of God. Then you can say, "I've got this", and mean it.

Romans 12:1-2: *I beseech you therefore brethren, by the mercies of God, that ye present your bodies a living sacrifice, holy, acceptable unto God, which is your reasonable service. Be not conformed to this world, but be ye transformed by the renewing of your mind, that ye may prove what is that good, and acceptable and perfect will of God.*

This scripture states to present your bodies a living sacrifice - holy, acceptable unto God. That's your reasonable service, the very least you could do, considering all that He has done for you. Looking at this, you might say times have changed, but God's Word remains the same. Don't be conformed to this world that we're living in where everybody's having sex. Abstinence is not being talked about. When we do what everybody is doing, sleeping around, man-to-man, woman-to-woman, we are conforming to this present world. Being transformed is a process. You might say, "Can I do this"?

The answer is yes, you can renew your mind! The scripture says by the renewing of your mind, which is continual work. Isn't it strange that you can be sitting right in the church and be a million miles away? Your body is present, yet your mind is gone and not focused on the Lord. Don't act deep... somebody say Amen!

This happens to all of us, but our choice of action is another book. No certain place, no certain time, it just happens. It's like a pop-up on your computer screen, you click it and it goes away, only to come back over and over and over again. You can use your pop-up blocker on the computer to solve the problem. The same is with our mind. Thoughts and images come and we mentally click it, to go away, only to come right back. All thoughts are not bad thoughts, but just not the right timing. So as it is in the natural - it is in the spirit. Use your pop-up blocker, which in this case is God's Word. Do our hormones realize that we are in church, do our hormones know that is a married man and do they know that we're trying to suppress them? Sometimes it just does not work!!!!!!!! You must change your mind to think on other things. The Bible says resist the devil and he will flee. Many times we are overpowered by them (thoughts) and end up where we said we would never be again. Sitting under fresh rhema Word (spoken Word) getting fresh and new illumination from the shepherd (Pastor) and all of a sudden, the mind wanders off to yonder place. It has nothing to do with the Word or the church, as a matter of fact, you just "left the building", physically, while still present. The Bible says, "as a man thinketh, so is he". So, at this point, rather than letting our minds run rampant, we change our thinking,

"Processing Out" or organizing our thoughts. Just start thinking on the goodness of Jesus, and all He's done for you, at that point your soul should start crying hallelujah, thank you, God for saving me. For sure that will change your thinking

Phil. 4:8: Finally, brethren, whatsoever things are true, whatsoever things are honest, whatsoever things are just, whatsoever things are pure, whatsoever things are lovely, whatsoever things are of good report, if there be any virtue, and if there be any praise, think on these things.

The word finally means: *the end result of a succession or process.* In order to get the result you want, your thinking has got to be on pure things. We plot to get what we want. After all, what the heart wants, the heart wants regardless of the fact that we could be ruining lives – both our own and others.

There is no shame in the game, unless the lord sends *conviction*. Conviction - what does this mean? **Con·vic·tion**: *being shown to be at fault resulting in a godly sense of guilt/remorse*. Conviction leaves an impression with a sense of guilt. Eventually, you will regret all those actions and thoughts.

A strong conviction will cause you to run from a thing and not to a thing. You must have a heart of pursuing God and his righteousness. It is not an overnight wonder, nor a miracle, but a process. I know that's right! This means you have to look at the real you - not the false, pretending you, or the "made up" you. Not you that everybody sees, but you who is open and honest, who says "I'm a mess, but I'm working on me." Then you learn to deal with every part and every issue of you, no one else, just you. I'm by no means saying it is easy or a piece of cake. It's a struggle. It's hard work.

For example, a couple walking and holding hands, seeing the couple's love for one another, or a friend that says, "I have to go, my husband or wife is at home." These can trigger a "why not me" time, that I call spazzation. Spazzing out… what's wrong with me? Why not me? Why can't that be me? Why can't I be married and happy?

This is the time the devil will speak to you and encourage you to engage in a relationship that will not be healthy, nor will it make you whole or happy. Let's look at "happy". It is based on what's happening around you, your situation and/or circumstance. For some women, this would cause low self-esteem, overeating, self-pity, oppression, and depression. Your mind at that time read something that may be so far from the truth that it's pathetic.

We think all the good men and women are taken, but rest assured, God is working on your man or woman. So you have a chance of having a designer man or woman. All our needs are different, but God is a strategic planner.

John 10:10 *the thief cometh not, but for to steal, and to kill, and to destroy: I am come that they might have life, and that they might have it more abundantly.*

The thief comes to steal your pure thoughts, to kill the things of good rapport, to corrupt the things that are honest and lovely. Abundant life is when nothing is missing and nothing is broken… the Shalom of God, His peace. When considering the word wholeness, healthy comes to mind. Growing, nourishing and thriving. All these components make up a God-desired relationship. *That's* a real relationship.

3 John 1:2 Beloved, I wish above all things that thou mayest prosper and be in health, even as thy soul prospereth.

Frequently, we live a lie - pretending. We can be the best actors. Not by doing all the giving and/or all the taking, but where each person plays a role and does whatever is needed at the time. Our emotions can be a roller coaster ride, up today, down today, complete with curves and twists.

But we as children of the Almighty, must rely on God and God alone.

Prov. 3:6 *In all your ways acknowledge him, and he shall direct your paths.*

Ask God. Only He knows the who's, what's, why's and where's of our lives. If you give the best you, then you can receive the best man or woman.

Gal. 6:7: *Be not deceived. God is not mocked: for whatsoever a man soweth, that shall he also reap.*

This applies to life as a whole. When you give your best, then you will receive the best. This scripture applies to everything in life. It is called the law of reciprocity. Many times in our lives, we think so deeply - needing a deep revelation on everything. All things are already revealed. There is no hidden mystery to anything. Sometimes it is what it is.

We over analyze things that keep us afraid of the "what ifs." But "what if" you are wrong and make a misjudgment because you over thought or over analyzed the situation and fear set in. All relationships are not, nor will be the same. If you have learned from the past, let go of all the ties of the past.

Phil 3:13-14: *Brethren, I count not myself to have apprehended: but this one thing I do, forgetting those things which are behind, and reaching forth unto those things which are before, I press toward the mark for the prize of the high calling of God in Christ Jesus.*

Your past should not keep you hostage. Forgetting is step one, and then reaching is step two. When these two things are done, you are on your way towards the mark, for it is a high calling. Change has got to come in order to receive the prize. Be mature and move beyond all that past stuff.

2 Tim. 1:7: *For God hath not given us the spirit of fear but of power, and of love, and of a sound mind.*

Use the power that you possess to overcome your fears. Fear will keep you looking back, holding you hostage. When that happens, you miss what is right in front of you. Have a sound mind about things in life. When thinking of soundness, the word stable comes to mind. Be stable in your thinking, not backward and forward. Use what God has given us, which is power, love and a sound mind.

James 1:8: *A double minded man is unstable in all his ways.*

Chapter 5

"What Is Your Name?

Most of the time, women look for a good man, but men look for a good woman also. Be that good woman - a woman of God that prays and intercedes for her family. What you present is what you receive.

Luke 6:38: *Give, and it shall be given unto you, good measure, pressed down, and shaken together, and running over, shall men give into your bosom.*

For with the same measure that ye meet withal it shall be measured to you again. Be a woman of faith. It will lead you into His perfect plan. Ruth met her Boaz. The Bible never says that Ruth was looking for a man. It says that she was working and Boaz saw her. Let's get some things straight. A Boaz is not broke, not unattractive, but a gentleman, impressively business-minded and knows how to treat a lady.

The question that comes to mind is what made Ruth so special that she just walked right into her destiny. All Ruth was doing was following her leader.

Prov. 2:21: *A good name is rather to be chosen than great riches, and loving favor rather than silver and gold.*

This scripture speaks volumes to me personally. I made the decision to get and keep a good name. You must realize - men talk. There's no way that your name won't precede you, the good, the bad and the ugly. This goes for both men and women.

So now you are saved and living for Christ. People always remember what you have done. Most of the time they don't forget and they make sure they remind you by telling you the "I remember when" stories. By the grace of God, you are a new creature, old things are passed away, all things are new.

Thank God for new mercy and grace.

2 Cor. 5:17: *Therefore if any man be in Christ, he is a new creature: old things are passed away, behold, all things are become new.*

I want to thank Him right now for keeping me through the struggle, He is a keeper. That memorable, romantic night that was full of bliss and passion, a time when you thought it just can't get any better yes, that night. But choose. Make your choices wisely, based on the Word of God.

Gal. 6:9: *And let us not be weary in well doing: for in due season we shall reap, if we faint not.*

Don't get tired of doing the right thing. After long periods of time we can get discouraged and start thinking what's the use. Now that I'm a single person, I remember the good times more than the bad, because good always outweighs bad.

Now I use this time to encourage my friends and family to try and hold it together, because once you separate or divorce, there will be bleeding and then a time of healing - because half of you has been cut away. The healing process can be long and you can become vulnerable. For an example, if you were married for 20 years, in 2 weeks don't think you're ok, because you're not. Typically men will suppress their feelings and emotions men can move on, but women are such emotional beings and need more time to heal. I ask my friends "When things go wrong in your relationship, are you sure you're ready for singleness?" That's usually my question. I share my experience with them, then I ask again. Are you sure? Are you prepared? Personally, I don't think anyone can handle the lifestyle of being single and saved without really depending on God. There's no way you can do it alone. If you think you can, you set yourself up for failure.

Stay out of situations and circumstances that will cause you to have a name change. Don't take the word "Saved" lightly – it's Saved and no sex. Saved and no midnight rendezvous. Saved and sex life on lock down. It takes a real woman to go from marriage to nothing. That's why we must go from marriage to the relying on God. Oftentimes we plan, but we can't go through with it on our own. Sometimes God intervenes. God has a master plan for your life that only He knows.

Jer. 29:11: *For I know the thoughts that I think toward you, says the LORD, thoughts of peace, and not of evil, to give you an expected end.*

So don't get overwhelmed and make wrong choices. When the time is right, things will fall in place. You are not entirely spiritual. You are human. What is your name? Your name says a lot. Even more importantly, what do men call you? Even Jesus asked the question of His disciples, "whom do men say that I am?'

Mark 8:27: *And Jesus went out, and his disciples, into the towns of Caesarea Philippi: and by the way he asked his disciples, saying unto them, Whom do men say that I am?*

Your name is Ruth, saved, sanctified, Holy Ghost-filled, Child of God. If you are called out of the name that God calls you, you should not answer. Take your choice. The good news is that God Almighty has an expected end. His plan towards you is only good.

As previously stated we are tri-beings; mind, body and soul. *"The mind and body communicate constantly. What the mind thinks, perceives, and experiences is sent from our brain to the rest of the body."* Herbert Benson, M.D., Institute for Mind Body Medicine.

Eph. 4:14 : *that we henceforth be no more children, tossed to and fro, and carried about with every wind of doctrine, by the sleight of men, and cunning craftiness, whereby they lie in wait to deceive.*

Let's grow up in our minds and not be children or babes. God gave His Word, which is a sure foundation. It's accurate information. Thoughts will shape who you are and your emotions.

Don't let your thoughts control your feelings. Get your mind and emotions together through the Word of God. The mind is a thought life and the place where Satan assaults us. He's always waiting to deceive.

Rom. 8:6-8: *For to be carnally minded is death, but to be spiritually minded is life and peace. Because the carnal mind is enmity against God: for it is not subject to the law of God, neither indeed can be. So then they that are in the flesh cannot please God.*

Having a fleshly mind is against God and eventually causes death. But a spiritual mind will cause a peaceful life. God says, "Let this mind be in you." The mind is where the battle goes on.

Phil 2:5 Let this mind be in you, which was also in Christ Jesus.

When I think of this scripture, I think of Christ's mind. His mind has no evil, only loving thoughts because He is a loving God. He has unconditional love for you. Whenever we decide to do good, evil is always present. Who do you let control your mind?

A strong weapon Satan uses against the Christian is the sexual demon. We get beat up in that arena. Satan makes us his slave, and then we react to the works of the flesh. We need the character of Christ, which is the fruit of the spirit.

Eph. 2:3-4: *Among whom also we all had our conversation in times past in the lusts of our flesh, fulfilling the desires of the flesh and of the mind, and were by nature the children of wrath, even as others. But God, who is rich in mercy, for his great love wherewith he loved us,*

In reality the mind is fleshly, which is carnal. Obey the spirit. Do what you know is right based on the Word of God. Sin should have no dominion over you.

2 Cor. 10-4: *For the weapons of our warfare are not carnal, but mighty through God to the pulling down of strong holds,*

A strong hold is persistent and contrary to the Word of God. (Casting down imaginations) Imagination comes from the root word imagine. It's a picture that you get in your mind. You have to learn how to control every imagination or image.

What you allow yourself to think about will eventually happen. Mental activity becomes physical activity. In the spirit, you can think about defeat or victory. What stays in your thoughts will enter into your spirit. When we become involved in sin, we visualize it first, and then we act on it. If you are victorious in your mind, the physical victories will follow. We are free-willed, so the choice is ours. But our desire to please God should outweigh our carnal wants and desires… meaning put God first.

Prov. 3:6: *In all thy ways acknowledge Him, and He shall direct thy paths.*

Direction is needed for many things in life, from simple to complex. Ask God. He will guide you into all truth. If we walk according to the spirit, then we won't fulfill the lust of the flesh. The lust of the flesh is nothing trivial because it demands your attention.

Instead of allowing your thoughts to focus on that, refocus on the things and the principles of God, not on finding a perfect, ideal, romantic relationship. Stay focused on the purpose and the destiny that God has planned for your life. Focus now becomes key. Key - just like ordinary keys that unlock locked doors in life, you need the key to unlock things in the mind. God's Word will help you to adjust and redirect your attention to more than just yourself. When adjusting your attention and energy on serving the Lord, He has the perfect outcome.

We want to be swept off our feet by a handsome prince or beautiful princess and God is preparing you just for him or her. Your mindset has to be able to handle a prince or princess. You have to be royal and not common. The prince or princess has high values and standards, and that's what is expected of you. Step up your game - it increases your value. The Bible lets us know that we are fearfully and wonderfully made.

Ps. 139:14 *I will praise thee, for I am fearfully and wonderfully made: marvelous are thy works, and that my soul knoweth right well.*

This means you are the best, and you should expect the best. With that said, depression, low self-esteem, poor stewardship, oppression: (the state of being subjected to such treatment or control) have no place in your life. As the scripture stated previously, you are fearfully and wonderfully made, get it in your spirit and let your spirit talk to your mind.

Chapter 6

"Ageless"

You might be saying to yourself you're an older woman, but trust me, it does not matter. In fact, no one is excluded from the Word, whether you are in your 20's, 30's, 40's or 50's, you are not excluded. The Word is for the young as well as the old.

Gen. 17:15-17: And God said unto Abraham, As for Sarai thy wife, thou shalt not call her name Sarai, but Sarah shall her name be. And I will bless her, and give thee a son also of her: yea, I will bless her, and she shall be a mother of nations, kings of people shall be of her. Then Abraham fell upon his face, and laughed, and said in his heart, Shall a child be born unto him that is an hundred years old? and shall Sarah, that is ninety years old, bear?

The promise was made and it was ageless. No time limit, no expiration date, just a promise. Imagine if Abraham and Sarah were excluded because of their ages. There is no different Bible for different age groups.

More than likely, it was not on the first try that Sarah conceived. No matter how young or old, the principle of having sex is based on God's Word. Frequently we are so casual about our behavior. That's what concerns me in this 21st century. We must consider and be mindful that our body is where the spirit lives.

1 Cor. 6:19-20: *What? Know ye not that your body is the temple of the Holy Ghost which is in you, which ye have of God, and ye are not your own? [20]For ye are bought with a price: therefore glorify God in your body, and in your spirit, which are God's.*

Honor God with your body. Don't be fooled. God will bless you for walking out His Word. We find ourselves talking about the Word. Let's not keep talking but keep walking. Make this a two-fold deal - walk and talk.

When we do this, we honor God with our words and actions. This seems overwhelming at times, even impossible. However, it can be done.

With God all things are possible. Redirection now comes into play. Start praying and cry out to God. Be honest, open, and express your feelings to Him.

1Thess. 5:22-23: *Abstain from all appearance of evil and the very God of peace shall sanctify you wholly, and I pray God your whole spirit and soul and body be preserved blameless unto the coming of our Lord Jesus Christ.*

Abstain from the very appearance of evil. If the situation looks bad, at all costs stay away. Abstain is the root of the word abstinence. **The meaning of abstain:** *by one's choice not to do something.* Wow! Abstain, abstinence. Many people have made the choice to live an abstinent life. On the other hand, what I find so ironic is that most Christians don't practice abstinence. When you don't practice abstinence, then you step out of the arch of safety.

When you're not under the covering, it opens up all kinds of turmoil, hardships and demonic attachments. The Bible says, the very God of peace sanctifies you wholly, which means set apart, different. Then God takes your whole spirit, soul and body and preserves it blameless until he comes back. Look not only at the surface but deeper. God sets you apart, and then he keeps you so that no one can blame you till he comes to get you. All of this takes place when you abstain.

1 Cor. 7:2 : *Nevertheless, to avoid fornication, let every man have his own wife, and let every woman have her own husband.*

Abraham and Sarah were married. Sarah was 99 and he was 100. But sex has no age limit. If you are unmarried and indulge in sex, then you are considered a fornicator, which is a sin. To avoid fornication let every man have his own wife, and every woman have her own husband.

Heb. 13:4: *Marriage is honorable in all, and the bed undefiled: but whoremongers and adulterers God will judge.*

Defile means to make something unclean, degrade, to corrupt the purity of something. The marriage bed is pure, holy and clean. Outside marriage and having sex, God will be your judge. How does He judge? According to His Word. The latter clause of the above scripture states: but whoremonger and adulterer, God will judge. God is just and fair based on what He said. I'm so glad God is my judge. He is also called the righteous judge.

Isaiah 103:5*: Who satisfies your mouth with good things, so that your youth is renewed like the eagles.*

Don't grow impatient because of age, but wait patiently. He is a restorer of all that may have been lost. He will renew your youth, vitality, and strength and will make you energetic and vigorous.

Ps.27:5: *For in the time of trouble He shall hide me in His pavilion: in the secret of His tabernacle shall He hide me, He shall set me up upon a rock.*

Thank God for a hiding place, a place of safety, a covering and a place of refuge. When I'm feeling lonely, I hide out in His pavilion. When I feel overwhelmed with temptation, I challenge myself to a day of nothing but His Word, through DVD's or CD's or just reading the Bible. Therefore I find myself in the secret of His tabernacle, where I am safe.

Chapter 7

Reward

Rev. 3:11 *Behold, I come quickly: hold that fast which thou hast, that no man takes thy crown.*

When I think of reward, I think of getting a trophy for an accomplishment, of being rewarded for meeting and making a goal. Goals are used as a gauge for measuring our success. I'm not saying it's always easy, sometimes goals are hard to reach. But keep striving, let no man take your crown, and by all means don't just give it away.

Ps. 84:11: *For the LORD God is a sun and shield: the LORD will give grace and glory: no good thing will He withhold from them that walk uprightly.*

Go ahead, set your goals. My goal is no sex before marriage. It is attainable. No cheating when I do get married - it can be done. Being 100% whole while I'm single. There are all kinds of awards: musical, athletic, noble, and academic awards to name a few.

But the greatest award is being able to hear God say, "Well done, thy good and faithful servant, enter into the joy of the Lord." Don't lose heart, hang on. Jesus Christ is both our reward and the rewarder. There is a reward for being upright… remember Job.

Job 1:1 : *There was a man in the land of Uz, whose name was Job, and that man was perfect and upright, and one that feared God, and eschewed evil.*

Gal 6:9: *And let us not be weary in well doing: for in due season we shall reap, if we faint not.*

Christians, we have more than just four seasons in the natural. We have a fifth season, which is our due season - our rightful time of blessings. Don't faint, keep fighting. You will not only get a heavenly reward, but you will also receive the reward of peace of mind, not having to deal with unwanted pregnancies, sexually transmitted diseases and/or HIV/AIDS.

In exchange for the satisfaction of the flesh, you leave the covering, you forsake His principles and you step out of His Word. Now you need Him to heal and restore you. But don't worry because He's a rewarder of those that diligently seek Him, for those of us who continually seek God, night and day, over and over again. To be recognized to receive an award is fantastic. Living with Christ is in itself is a reward. Although you may not receive earthly fame or earthly glory, surely your reward is heaven.

To receive a reward from God - wow… that's better than any Oscar or Grammy Award. Rewarded by the God of all creation!

Chapter 8

"Girl Talk"

If we had someone to talk to and tell us the truth, we would be more apt to do better. Sometimes, we hide behind lies and/or deceit, but the truth is just the truth. Men don't really want an easy woman. In years past, an easy woman was called a "round-the-way" woman. That's not the category we want to find ourselves in. The category we want to be in is the "take home to mama" woman. All I'm saying is don't give it up so quickly and so easily. For some it is ridiculously easy—the man doesn't even have to work for it. You have to demand respect if you want respect. If he's a man, you are worth the wait to him, but if he's a boy, he'll go play.

1 Cor. 13:11 *When I was a child, I spake as a child, I understood as a child, I thought as a child: but when I became a man, I put away childish things.*

Know this, you are nobody's slave, nobody's fool, and nobody's punching bag. An old saying is "Why buy the cow, when you can get the milk for free?" Then a man takes the milk and makes ice cream in all flavors and that's just too much. Have you seen the price of milk today? It is by no means free. It's expensive. Make him pay the price, not being a gold-digger, but through the principles of the Word. Women are helpmeets, not the head of the house.

You are to help the man (and the men say, "Amen"). If they didn't need help, then women wouldn't be called the help meet. You are called the helpmeet by God almighty.

Gen. 2:18 The Lord God said, "It is not good for the man to be alone. I will make a helper suitable for him."

From a woman's point of view, there's nothing like having a good man. Our idea is a perfect man… there's no such thing.

Perfect man or perfect woman, neither of them exists. But a man or woman that God is still working on, is an ideal man or woman. We are all pressing towards the mark of the prize of the high calling.

Phil. 3:14 *I press toward the mark for the prize of the high calling of God in Christ Jesus.*

So, woman, be patient. Hold on and keep high standards. This is a scenario, for example, a "round the way" kind of woman and the "high standard, trustworthy, integritous" woman. Which one would you choose to marry or just to engage in night of pleasure? Step into a man's shoes and decide.

If you chose the one to marry, then you realize you need someone that's trustworthy and honest. Are you looking to have a good time with no strings attached? But strings ARE ALWAYS attached in more ways than one.

If you chose the one-night stand, you chose the woman without standards in place. You got exactly what you wanted. Why desire a King, if you're not Queen status? Why desire a Prince, if you're not Princess status? Ladies, we've got to get those values and morals up. Relationships are hard work and require lots of unselfish time. A woman can spot out a trashy woman, because that's what a good woman tries not to be. It shows in conversation, dress, and in honesty. Choose to be classy, not trashy. Let's not keep talking about it, but let's be what God has called and also predestined. God is a God of excellence and we should be striving to be just like Him in all aspects of life. The saying is "A woman knows another woman" meaning you can identify stereotypical traits. When you love someone, love shows. You can't deny it, you can't hide it and guess what, it is obvious to those around you. Love speaks for itself. Jesus gave His life because He loved us.

John 3:16 *For God so loved the world, that He gave His only begotten Son, that whosoever believeth in him will not perish, but have everlasting life.*

A secret love won't work. Everyone around you will know, you can't see that everyone else is aware. Love is so strong that you can't hide it. If you are trustworthy, that will shut down all insecurities. Surely he or she is insecure because of past relationships, so you want a fresh, open, honest, relationship where you can be trusted wholeheartedly.

Prov. 31:11: *The heart of her husband doth safely trust in her, so that he shall have no need of spoil.*

For an example, in all past relationships he has encountered trust issues. The problem is that he is scared due to past trust issues. He needs to be able to fully trust in you. That's when your character and integrity step up and save the day. You can use the track record of your lifestyle to prove your case of good character. Let's say something does come up from your past about your character. Then you can say let's look at the track record. Looking at it should help the partner to be secure and remove doubt. Trust is a big issue in any relationship.

Chapters 9

Do's

Areas we can work

on while waiting:

Dos:

1. **Be wise and use wisdom.**

    ❖ Use knowledge and experience to make your choices.

2. **Dress appropriately at all times.**

    ❖ Personal hygiene is a must!
    ❖ Don't be too revealing and under dressed.

3. **Be honest.**

    ❖ Share the real you - your wants and desires and let him share his, make a point to share similar things and/or what the both of you have in common.

4. **Carry yourself like a lady**

    ❖ A must...at all times. When you carry yourself like a lady it is attractive to men.

5. **Be independent.**

    ❖ Be able to pay your own rent, car payments, and take care of yourself.

6. **Be classy.**

    ❖ Behaving in a suitable way, regardless of the situation.

7. **Be confident.**

    ❖ Believe in yourself

8. **Be seen and not heard.**

    ❖ Be Soft spoken, not loud and obnoxious.

9. **Be selective of your environment.**

    ❖ Know where you are going, no surprises.

10. Be specific.

❖ Make everything clear, nobody should have to guess and try to get it right. No one should have to try and read your mind.

Chapter 10

Dont's

Don'ts:

1. **Don't forsake God.**

   ❖ Forsake any and everything else, but always keep your trust in God - He has never failed.

2. **Don't settle.**

   ❖ Settling is not really what you want, so in order to get what you want just wait. Special orders take time

3. **Don't advertise.**

   ❖ Don't carry the sign that you are for sale - you are not.

4. **Don't be hasty with love.**

   ❖ Take your time and walk into love. If you fall in love, then you can fall out of love.[iii]

5. **Don't be hasty with sex – (preferably NO sex)**

    ❖ Need I say more? The act of sex is reserved for married people.

6. **Don't be wasteful with your time, money, etc.**

    ❖ Again, be wise. Don't waste time or throw money away. Be a good steward of both.

7. **Don't be passive.**

    ❖ Make people prove themselves.

8. **Don't talk too much or too little.**

    ❖ Both of these can be a turn off. Find a happy medium and common ground.

9. **Don't be arrogant.**

    ❖ Don't have an exaggerated sense of your own importance or abilities.

10. **Don't ask for too much.**

    ❖ Don't ask for hair, nails, cars, homes, etc. - Be large and in charge.

Scripture References

"So then faith cometh by hearing, and hearing by the Word of God."

Romans 10:17

Gen. 1:27 *So God created man in His own image, in the image of God created he him, male and female created he them*

Gen 2:8 *And the LORD God planted a garden eastward in Eden, and there He put the man whom He had formed.*

Gen 2:21-22 *And the LORD God caused a deep sleep to fall upon Adam, and he slept: and He took one of his ribs, and closed up the flesh instead thereof, And the rib, which the LORD God had taken from man, made Him a woman, and brought her unto the man.*

Gen 2:23 *And Adam said, This is now bone of my bones, and flesh of my flesh: she shall be called Woman, because she was taken out of Man.*

John 10:10 *The thief cometh not, but for to steal, and to kill, and to destroy: I am come that they might have life, and that they might have it more abundantly.*

2 Cor. 6:14 *Be ye not unequally yoked together with unbelievers: for what fellowship hath righteousness with unrighteousness? and what communion hath light with darkness?*

Gen 2:22-24 *And the LORD God caused a deep sleep to fall upon Adam, and he slept: and he took one of his ribs, and closed up the flesh instead thereof, And the rib, which the LORD God had taken from man, made him a woman, and brought her unto the man. And Adam said, this is now bone of my bones, and flesh of my flesh: she shall be called Woman, because she was taken out of Man. Therefore shall a man leave his father and his mother, and shall cleave unto his wife: and they shall be one flesh.*

Ps. 27:14 *Wait on the LORD: be of good courage, and He shall strengthen thine heart: wait, I say, on the LORD.*

Phil. 4:11-13 *Not that I speak in respect of want: for I have learned, in whatsoever state I* am, therewith to be content. I know both how to be abased, and I know how to abound: every where and in all things I am instructed both to be full and to be hungry, both to abound and to suffer need. I can do all things through Christ who strengthens me.

2 Cor. 10:5 *Casting down imaginations, and every high thing that exalteth itself against the knowledge of God, and bringing into captivity every thought to the obedience of Christ.*

Romans 12:1-2 *I beseech you therefore brethren, by the mercies of God, that ye present your bodies a living sacrifice, holy, acceptable unto God, which is your reasonable service. Be not conformed to this world, but be ye transformed by the renewing of your mind, that ye may prove what is that good, and acceptable and perfect will of God.*

Phil. 4:8 *Finally, brethren, whatsoever things are true, whatsoever things are honest, whatsoever things are just, whatsoever things are pure, whatsoever things are lovely, whatsoever things are of good report, if there be any virtue, and if there be any praise, think on these things.*

John 10:10 *The thief cometh not, but for to steal, and to kill, and to destroy: I am come that they might have life, and that they might have it more abundantly.*

3 John 1:2 *Beloved, I wish above all things that thou mayest prosper and be in health, even as thy soul prospereth*

Ps. 3:6 *In all your ways acknowledge Him, and He shall direct your paths.*

Gal. 6:7 *Be not deceived, God is not mocked: for whatsoever a man soweth, that shall he also reap.*

Phil 3:13-14 *Brethren, I count not myself to have apprehended: but this one thing I do, forgetting those things which are behind, and reaching forth unto those things which are before, I press toward the mark for the prize of the high calling of God in Christ Jesus.*

2 Tim. 1:7 *For God hath not given us the spirit of fear, but of power, and of love, and of a sound mind.*

James 1:8 *A double minded man is unstable in all his ways.*

Luke 6:38 *Give, and it shall be given unto you, good measure, pressed down, and shaken together, and running over, shall men give into your bosom.*

Prov. 2:21 *A good name is rather to be chosen than great riches, and loving favor rather than silver and gold.*

2 Cor. 5:17 *Therefore if any man be in Christ, he is a new creature: old things are passed away, behold, all things are become new.*

Gal. 6:9 *And let us not be weary in well doing: for in due season we shall reap, if we faint not.*

Jer. 29:11 For *I know the thoughts that I think toward you, says the LORD, thoughts of peace, and not of evil, to give you an expected end.*

Eph. 4:14 That we henceforth be no more children, tossed to and fro, and carried about with every wind of doctrine, by the sleight of men, and cunning craftiness, whereby they lie in wait to deceive.

Isa. 6:23 That we henceforth be no more children, tossed to and fro, and carried about with every wind of doctrine, by the sleight of men, and cunning craftiness, whereby they lie in wait to deceive,

Rom. 8:6-8: *For to be carnally minded is death, but to be spiritually minded is life and peace. Because the carnal mind is enmity against God: for it is not subject to the law of God, neither indeed can be. So then they that are in the flesh cannot please God*

Phil 2:5 *Let this mind be in you, which was also in Christ Jesus.*

Eph. 2:3-4 *among whom also we all had our conversation in times past in the lusts of our flesh, fulfilling the desires of the flesh and of the mind, and were by nature the children of wrath, even as others. But God, who is rich in mercy, for His great love wherewith He loved us,*

2 Cor. 10-4 *For the weapons of our warfare are not carnal, but mighty through God to the pulling down of strong holds*

Prov. 3:6 *In all thy ways acknowledge Him, and He shall direct thy paths.*

Jer. 29:11 *For I know the thoughts that I think toward you, saith the LORD, thoughts of peace, and not of evil, to give you an expected end.*

Ps. 139:14 *I will praise thee, for I am fearfully and wonderfully made: marvelous are thy works, and that my soul knoweth right well.*

Gen. 17:15-17 *And God said unto Abraham, As for Sarai thy wife, thou shalt not call her name Sarai, but Sarah shall her name be. And I will bless her, and give thee a son also of her: yea, I will bless her, and she shall be a mother of nations, kings of people shall be of her. Then Abraham fell upon his face, and laughed, and said in his heart, Shall a child be born unto him that is an hundred years old? and shall Sarah, that is ninety years old, bear?*

1 Cor. 6:19-20 *What? Know ye not that your body is the temple of the Holy Ghost which is in you, which ye have of God, and ye are not your own? For ye are bought with a price: therefore glorify God in your body, and in your spirit, which are God's.*

1 Thess. 5:22-23 *Abstain from all appearance of evil. And the very God of peace sanctify you wholly, and I pray God your whole spirit and soul and body be preserved blameless unto the coming of our Lord Jesus Christ.*

1 Cor. 7:2 *Nevertheless, to avoid fornication, let every man have his own wife, and let every woman have her own husband.*

Heb. 13:4 *Marriage is honorable in all, and the bed undefiled: but whoremongers and adulterers God will judge.*

Isa. 103:5: *Who satisfies your mouth with good things, so that your youth is renewed like the eagles.*

Ps.27:5 *For in the time of trouble He shall hide me in His pavilion: in the secret of His tabernacle shall He hide me, He shall set me up upon a rock.*

Rev. 3:11 *Behold, I come quickly: hold that fast which thou hast, that no man take thy crown.*

Ps. 84 *For the LORD God is a sun and shield: the LORD will give grace and glory: no good thing will he withhold from them that walk uprightly.*

Gal 6:9 *And let us not be weary in well doing: for in due season we shall reap, if we faint not.*

1 Cor. 13:11: *When I was a child, I spake as a child, I understood as a child, I thought as a child: but when I became a man, I put away childish things.*

Gen. 2:18 *The L*ORD *God said, "It is not good for the man to be alone. I will make a*

Phil. 3:14 *I press toward the mark for the prize of the high calling of God in Christ Jesus.*

John 3:16 *For God so loved the world, that he gave his only begotten Son, that whosoever believeth in him should not perish, but have everlasting life.*

Prov. 31:11 *The heart of her husband doth safely trust in her, so that he shall have no need of spoil.*

*All scripture references are from the Holy Bible - King James Version- KJV "

_____

ACKNOWLEDGEMENTS :

1. DANNY SANTAGATO QUOTES
Being *single doesn't necessarily mean one is not wanted. In many cases it means that one knows what they want and if they can't find that someone special then they'll remain single forever because they're OK and happy with who they are and just want that someone special to complete them and take their happiness to a higher level.* WWW.DANNYSANTGATOQUOTES.COM

---

2. Dr. Kevin A. Williams: *"Take your time and walk into love. If you fall in love, then you can fall out of love."*

3. Herbert Benson, M.D., Institute for Mind Body Medicine: *"As previously stated we are tri- beings; mind, body and soul. "The mind and body communicate constantly. What the mind thinks, perceives, and experiences is sent from our brain to the rest of the body."*

www.ingramcontent.com/pod-product-compliance
Lightning Source LLC
LaVergne TN
LVHW051509070426
835507LV00022B/3002